STAGE 5 BOOK 6

RED FACES

Philippa Bateman

RISING STARS

Tasha ran into Club OK waving a copy of *Urban* magazine. Caleb and Maya were playing computer games but looked up when they heard Tasha.

"Get yourselves over here and check this out," she shouted.
"Tasha fusses about everything," smiled Caleb.

Tasha flicked to the gossip page and showed it to her friends. "It's K-Zee. He's the best!" she said.

"He's amazing," sighed Maya. "I've got two of his songs."

"I've liked his music for ages. I think I look like him," said Caleb. "Ha! In your dreams," laughed Maya.

"If you saw me in my dark glasses you'd think I was his twin," joked Caleb.

"Just read what it says," yelled Tasha.

"K-Zee comes from Dockside and his family still live there. He plans to return and star in the hit TV series, Celebrities, Buddies and Studies," read Caleb.

6

"What's that all about?" asked Maya.

"It's famous people who find their old mates and talk about what they were like at school," said Tasha.

"Quick, let's check out K-Zee's website," said Maya.

7

"I've found K-Zee's website!" shouted Caleb. Seconds later, Caleb yelled, "K-Zee is visiting Dockside today!"
The girls started screaming.

Oz heard them. "Ladies, be kind to my ears!" he joked. They showed him the website. "I went to school with K-Zee's dad in the nineties," said Oz.

"Is that the 1890s? That was ages ago!" said Maya.

"His dad and I were best buddies!" said Oz.
"Best buddies? Sweet!" said Maya.
"Thanks!" said Oz, grinning.

13

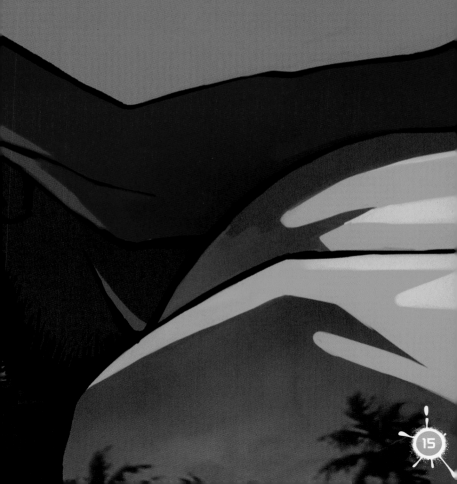

"I follow K-Zee's posts on his blog too.
I could tell you some funny stories ..."
"Oz, we'll laugh at your stories later.
Do you think you can get him to come
to Club OK?" said Tasha.

Oz agreed to contact K-Zee's dad.
"Tell him that we're K-Zee's
biggest fans," called Tasha.
"And see if we can go to one of
K-Zee's wild parties," said Maya.

"Just calm yourselves!" laughed Oz.

"I want to see his cars," said Caleb.
"I've heard he buys cars as if they were toys," added Tasha.
"I hope he replies," said Maya.

They did not see K-Zee and his dad come through the back door.

K-Zee used his phone to update his blog.

Hi. I'm at Club OK with my new best buddies.

Tasha, Maya and Caleb read the new post on K-Zee's blog. Then they saw K-Zee. They all screamed.
"Why do my fans always do that?" laughed K-Zee.

The fans blushed. Oz grinned.
"Red faces! Sweet!"